The Little
Munch

Catherine de Duve

**KATE'ART
EDITIONS**

Edvard at 2 years old

Edvard Munch was born on 12th December 1863 in Løten, in the county of Hedmark in Norway. The Munch family settled in a poor area of Kristiania, the capital, which changed its name to Oslo in 1924.

His father, Doctor Christian Munch, was a medical officer. He and his wife, Laura Cathrine, had five children, Sophie, Edvard, Andreas, Laura and Inger Marie. Sadly, when Edvard was only five years old, his mother became very poorly and died of tuberculosis. The little boy felt empty and abandoned. Home was a sad place to be. Everything was depressing.

Luckily for them, their mother's sister, Aunt Karen, came to live with them and brought joy back into their home.

Laura Cathrine with her children

From Home...

Aunt Karen taught her nieces and nephews and nieces to draw, paint and cut pretty silhouettes out of paper. She noticed and encouraged Edvard's talent. With the sale of her paintings, she bought painting material for her nephew and herself.

Edvard was a sickly child, so he was often home alone. He suffered from asthma and terrible rheumatism, but he made the most of his time on his own to do what he liked most: sit by the window and paint the landscape. In the distance he could see a church and houses covered in snow.

On some evenings, whilst sitting around the stove, Doctor Munch read them stories about goblins, trolls and scary ghosts, as well as Norwegian legends written by their Uncle Peter Andreas.
Edvard liked to paint his brothers, sisters, father and aunt. He also drew items around the house, interiors and his own hand.

Your turn! Paint or draw what you can see from your window just like Munch used to do.

Artist !

After a short stint at technical college to become an engineer to please his father, the eighteen year old Munch decided to become an artist. He entered the Royal School of Design and rented a studio with five of his friends. They all made the most of the precious advice Christian Krohg, the renowned *naturalist* painter, gave to them for free. He corrected and criticized their works and thanks to him, Munch exhibited for the first time at the Autumn Exhibition in 1883. He was all of 20 years old! Munch gained entry to the painter Fritz Thaulow's open air art studio where he painted the landscape.

❋ *The naturalists are artists (like Corot, Millet, Krogh and Thaulow) and writers (such as Zola, Tchekov, Ibsen and Strindberg) who reproduced reality in an objective manner based on an accurate depiction of detail.*

🔍 Make up a story that takes place in this realistic landscape.

His professor gave him a grant to enable him to perfect his training. Munch was over the moon! He could travel at last! "Hurray!, he shouted. Long live France! Let's wear out the floorboards at the Louvre until the state has to have them repainted!"

In the Spring of 1885 Munch left Norway for the first time. He was on his way to Paris. He went first to Antwerp in Belgium for the World's Fair. One of his works was on show. Here it is, who is she? His younger sister, Inger.

Sophie

Munch wanted to paint what no one could see, what he felt within himself, his emotions, fear, angst and chagrin. He mainly remembered the loss of loved ones and ill health. Years later he painted the memory of his mother, lying on her deathbed, deathly white. Visitors come to pay their last respects, the priest prays at her side, and her daughter Sophie, dressed in red, *grieves*. What gesture is she making? Could Munch be grieving through the act of painting?

✳ *Grief comes from Old French. It is the loss or intense sorrow caused by the death of a loved one. A family grieves the loss of a family member, coming to terms with the permanent nature of the separation.*

🔎 Have you already grieved for someone? Try to imagine how you would feel? Look for Sophie's gesture in another one of Munch's paintings.

Sophie was a sickly child. She is only 14 here, yet she just sits motionless in an armchair, a white pillow cushioning her head. She seems to be staring at a point in the distance which illuminates her. She will die soon. Who is the woman next to her? Edvard wept silently at her passing.

At the time, artists used to often depict sickbeds. Munch chose Betzy as a model and painted her sitting in Sophie's armchair. He kept going back to work on the painting, repainting it over and over again, scraping the paint, blotting it out, and starting over, scratching the canvas in the process. He wanted a hazy image, just as he remembered seeing his sister through his tears, the image etched in his mind.

The artist made a series of paintings using this same theme as well as numerous engravings. The public first saw the work in 1886 and was outraged, deeming it amateurish and unfinished. "What an amateur! An unfinished canvas!" No one understood the painful emotions Munch was expressing in this painting. Can you feel them?

Paris

In 1889, Munch had his first solo exhibition in Kristiania. Over 100 works or art were shown. But Paris was the place to be as far as the arts were concerned! He spent a lot of time there and met other artists, including the poet Stéphane *Mallarmé*. They became friends.

Mallarmé painted by Manet

Mallarmé *(1842-1898) was a French poet. One of his most famous poems is called: "A roll of the dice will never abolish chance". He wrote it like a drawing. It is a graphic poem.*

Compare the portrait painted by Manet to the one by Munch. Which do you prefer? Which one is called "The Absinthe Drinker"?

Manet, 1856   Munch, 1885

*To find out more, look for Long Live Impressionism and Pointillism! in the same collection.

10

Munch came across the impressionist and pointillist* painters in Paris. He used their technique. He was very impressed and inspired by Edouard Manet's full-length portraits, which became his first successful works.

Notice how lively Paris is.

The young artist spent the winter of 1891 in Nice in the South of France for his health. The beach, sky, sea, gardens in bloom, markets and passers-by became a new source of inspiration. But Edvard did not have enough money to live on. He had however heard of a game at the Monte-Carlo Casino and decided to try his luck.

The players choose a colour and a number on the green gaming table. "Place your bets. No further bets," the croupier shouts. The roulette spins around and everyone keeps their eyes riveted on the small ball that will settle on the winning number. In no time he was caught up in the game. "Red 2 as the winner!" Poor Munch, he had no luck.

🔍 Look at the people sitting at the roulette table.
What are they doing? Find the roulette and the croupier.

Fjords

The artist spent his summers in Asgardstrand, a small seaside town south of the Norwegian capital. He bought a fisherman's cottage there in 1897; the painted building was surrounded by a fenced garden. One year Edvard fell in love with a young girl he met there. They went on walks along the trails by the *fjords* and into the forest. Munch painted her in the semidarkness of the pinewoods. Her eyes are like round shadowy holes drawing us into the painting. The woman becomes a mystery. What is in the background?

❄ **A Fjord** *is an ancient and very deep glacial valley submerged by the sea. Fjords are often very long with high and craggy cliffs. The water is fresh since it comes from waterfalls and thawing snow. The depth of the water in these inlets of the sea is amongst the deepest in the world.*

Edvard met his friend Jappe one evening by the fjord. He was very sad and jealous because the woman he was in love with was with another. Munch depicted him with a bleeding heart, and the woman in white, drifting off dreamily like a ghost heading out to sea.

Draw the fjord towards which the woman is walking.

Vampire

Whilst walking down the very smart Karl-Johan Avenue, the 'Champs-Elysées' of Kristiania, Munch had a very strange feeling. Odd visions came to him. The promenade of the well healed had become a parade of spectres. The artist depicts them as pale wide-eyed zombies. These eerie masked figures move towards us in the freezing night. Brr....

🔍 Who are these people? Find Munch in the painting.

In 1892 Munch was invited to Berlin. The exhibition was a scandal and had to shut its doors after only one week! But the Norwegian artist, notoriously famous now, had made friends there and stayed in Germany for further exhibitions of his work.

🔍 Who is the vampire in this painting?

✏️ Draw a vampire or a ghost just like one of Munch's.

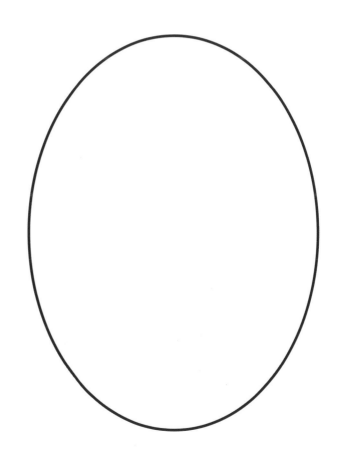

The Scream

I was out walking with two friends - the sun began to set - suddenly the sky turned blood red - I paused, feeling exhausted, and leaned on the fence - there was blood and tongues of fire above the blue-black fjord and the city - my friends walked on, and I stood there trembling with anxiety - and I sensed an endless scream passing through nature.

Edvard Munch

The colour seethes with movement, screaming and expressing itself. It is an explosive force as powerful as the human figure with its hands over its ears and its mouth wide open. It is screaming the existential angst of civilized man. "Free me from my fears!" Can you hear the scream?

Munch created several versions of The Scream. It is such a famous painting that it has been stolen twice from the Munch Museum, once in 1994 and a second time in 2004.

 Try to imagine what the figure is screaming.
Write it down or draw it.

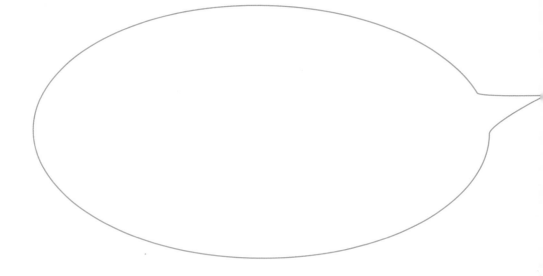

Midnight Sun

Munch returned to his homeland every summer. A particular phenomenon occurred at this time of year: the sun never set. He painted in the light of the *midnight sun* making the most of it.

What are the three girls doing on the bridge? Is it day or night? Where is the sun hiding itself? What time is it?

❄ *The midnight sun: Around the summer solstice (21st June in the northern hemisphere, 21st December in the southern hemisphere), in the areas close to the Arctic and Antarctic Circle, daylight lasts 24 hours! Night never falls those days! In the North, this phenomenon reaches its minimum (1 day) at the Polar Circle (66°34') and its maximum (6 months) at the Pole (90°). The nights are light and are called white nights.*

 Draw the midnight sun.

Expressionism

We know very little about Munch's private life. He met Tulla Larsen in 1898 but their relationship ended badly. Munch preferred to be alone with his painting. The artist had a nervous breakdown in 1908. He was consuming too much alcohol and was depressed. He needed help and had himself admitted to Copenhagen's psychiatric hospital in Denmark, where Doctor Jacobson treated him. Luckily, Edvard had a room with a studio. During his stay at the hospital where he continued to paint, his exhibitions were a success and he received the Royal Norwegian Order of St. Olav. The time in hospital did him a lot of good and a new life opened up to him.

Young artists, especially in Germany, were very influenced by Munch's work. For the expressionists who belonged to the *Die Brücke* group, the artist was a pioneer, a guide leading them towards a freer form of painting, modern painting.

Observe Dr Jacobson. Munch managed to express his main character trait.

What is it in your opinion? Is he self-assured, authoritarian or shy?

✳ ***Die Brücke*** *(The Bridge) was a group of German expressionist artists formed in Dresden in 1905. Kirchner, Heckel, Schmidt-Rottluff, Nolde... Emotions must be expressed. They employed a crude drawing technique using bold colours. They inspired themselves from primitivist art. Another expressionist group was formed in 1911 in Munich, it was called Der Blaue Reiter (The Blue Rider).*

village life

Look for this detail in the painting. It's your turn now to draw the outline of a figure.

Munch returned home on a steamboat. He would daydream on the deck looking out to sea. "Where am I going to settle?" He rented a house in Kragerø overlooking the sea. He loved looking at the sky, the clouds, the countryside, the trees... It was so much more pleasant than his anguished internal visions. He was very much at peace there and worked outside.
Children and ducks came to see him.

How many ducks can you see?

Giddy Up!

Panic! A horse pounds down the hill galloping out of control! "Careful children! Get out of the way!" the farmer yells from his cart. The horse's mane whips about, as he twists his head around with a wild look in his eyes. The combination of refined and powerful brush strokes suggests the wild speed of the horse. Can you feel the momentum?

Look closely at Munch's technique and place the details back where they belong.

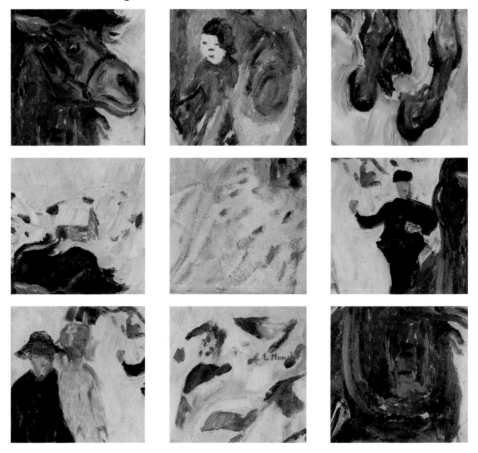

Starry Night

In 1912 his paintings were exhibited alongside works by Cézanne, Van Gogh and Gauguin. He becomes as well known as them. In 1916 he bought Ekely, a property near Kristiania. It had a large garden as well as fruit trees, horses, dogs, cows and pigs. A farm in other words! He loved the company of animals.

At night, from his terrace, Munch could see the city lights twinkling like stars.

His house was full of his canvases. Sometimes he even hung them on the trees outside to air them. What a funny idea! He always had to have his charcoal and paintbrushes with him just in case he had the urge to paint...

Munch often painted rounded shadows.
Search for them in the book.

Compare Munch's starry night (1924) on the left with Van Gogh's (1889) on the right. Can you spot any similarities?

The Frieze of Life

Munch had several outdoor studios built in his garden so he could work on a series he called "The Frieze of Life". It depicts his vision of love, angst and death. In 1937 Munch's paintings were considered *degenerate art* by the Nazis. His work was confiscated. He was very attached to his paintings so bought some back and copied others before selling them. The Second World War erupted and Norway was occupied by the Germans in 1940. Edvard refused all contact with the Nazis.

Munch often painted life and death. What do you think he was painting here? Life, death or both?

Edvard Munch died peacefully at home on 23rd January 1944, he was 81 years old. Munch's life's work amounts to thousands of works of art that he created with passion and donated to the town of Oslo upon his death. He is Norway's most renowned and exhibited artist.

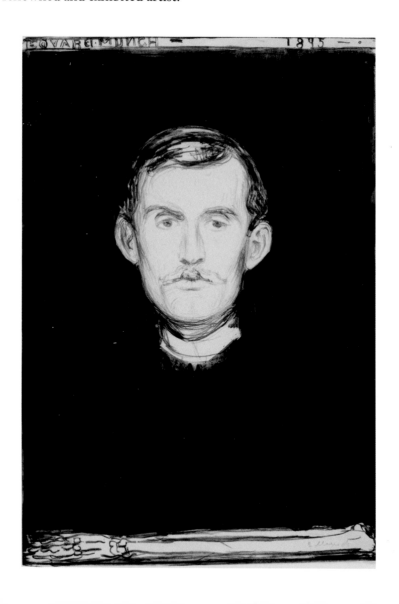

Text & illustration: Catherine de Duve
Concept & coordination: Kate'Art Editions
Graphic Design: Virginie Cornet & Carole Daprey
Translation: Kerry-Jane Lowery

OSLO
Munch Museum:
Summer Night. The Voice, 1896, oil on unprimed canvas, 90 x 119,5 cm: cover, p.14.
Self-Portrait, 1881-1882, oil on paper mounted on cardboard, 26 x 19 cm: p.1, p.6.
Karen Bjølstad in the Rocking Chair, 1883, oil on canvas, 47,5 x 41 cm: p.3.
Old Aker Church, 1881, oil on cardboard, 16 x 21 cm: p.4-5.
From Maridalen, 1881, oil on unprimed cardboard, 22 x 27,5 cm: p.6.
Death and the Child, 1899, oil on unprimed canvas, 104,5 x 179,5 cm: p.8.
At the Roulette Table in Monte Carlo, 1892, oil on canvas, 74,50 x 116 cm: p.12-13.
Separation, 1896, oil on canvas, 96,5 x 127 cm: p.15.
Dr. Daniel Jacobson, 1908-1909, oil on canvas, 204 x 111,5 cm: p.22-23.
Children and Ducks, 1906, oil on canvas, 100 x 105 cm: p.24-25.
Galloping Horse, 1910-1912, oil on canvas, 148 x 120 cm: p.26-27.
Starry Night, 1922-24, oil on canvas, 140 x 119 cm: p.28.
Self-portrait. Between the clock and the Bed, 1940-1943, oil on canvas, 149,5 x 120,5 cm: p.29.
The Sun, 1912, oil on canvas, 123 x 176,5 cm: p.30.
Self-portrait with Skeleton Arm, 1895, lithograph, 455-462 x 324 mm: p.31.
Copyright all photographs: Munch Museum
National Museum of Art, Architecture and Design:
The Scream, 1893, oil, tempera, and pastel on cardboard, 91 cm x 73,5 cm: cover, p.19.
Inger Munch in Black, 1884, oil on canvas, 97 x 67 cm: p.7.
The Sick Child, 1885-1886, oil on canvas, 119,5 x 118,5 cm: p.9.
Rue Lafayette, 1891, oil on canvas, 92 x 73 cm: p.11.
Girls on the Bridge, 1927, oil on canvas, 136 x 125,5 cm: p.20.
Private collection: *Portrait of Karl Jensen-Hjell*, 1885, oil on canvas, 190 x 100 cm: p.10.
Vampire, 1894, oil on canvas, 91 x 109 cm: p.17.
BERGEN
Bergen Art Museum: *Karl-Johann, The Evening*, 1892, oil on canvas, 84,5 x 121 cm: p.16-17.

PARIS
Musée d'Orsay: Manet, *Portrait of Mallarmé*, 1876: p.10.
COPENHAGEN
Ny Carlsberg Glyptotek: Manet, *Le Buveur d'absinthe*, 1856: p.11.
NEW YORK
MoMA: Van Gogh, *Starry Night*, 1889: p.29.

With thanks to : Frédérique Masquelier, Olivier Olbrechts, Letizia Rossi, Karen Lerheim, The Munch Museum, Andreas Harvik, Nasjonalmuseet, Christa Köressaar, Nasjonal Museet, Linda Klyve, Bergen Kunstmuseum, Tinne Billet, Sofam, Kari Astrup, BONO and everyone who helped to make this book.

Discover art while having fun !
Our books are available in English, French, German, Dutch and Spanish.
www.kateart.com